I Choose Happy

Come, Join Me

by
Wayne Williams

This book is a personal memoir. As such, it contains descriptions of events, places, persons and experiences as the author remembers or perceived them. Other witnesses may have different perspectives.

I CHOOSE HAPPY: COME, JOIN ME

Copyright © 2020 by Wayne Williams. All rights reserved, including the right to reproduce this book, or portions thereof, in any form. No part of this text may be reproduced, transmitted, downloaded, decompiled, reverse engineered, or stored in or introduced into any information storage and retrieval system, in any form or by any means, whether electronic or mechanical without the express written permission of the author. The scanning, uploading, and distribution of this book via the Internet or via any other means without the permission of the publisher is illegal and punishable by law. Please purchase only authorized electronic editions and do not participate in or encourage electronic piracy of copyrighted materials.

The publisher does not have any control over and does not assume any responsibility for author or third-party websites or their content.

Cover design by Telemachus Press, LLC and Jason Housby

Cover and interior images are the property of Wayne Williams or are used with permission.
The Optimist is reprinted with permission from Beryl MacDonald

Published by Telemachus Press, LLC
7652 Sawmill Road, Suite 304
Dublin, Ohio 43016
http://www.telemachuspress.com

ISBN# 978-1-951744-08-3 (paperback)

Library of Congress Control Number: 2020904223

Version 2020.07.03

Foreword
by Barbara A. Glanz

Wayne Williams has blessed my life beyond measure! Even though I have not yet met him in person, we have become friends of the heart and soul, and we both feel that God was the orchestrator of our finding one another. He is one of the most precious, godlike persons I have ever known. I just wish I could have known his wife, Rosie.

Our story began when Uncle Wayne, as he has asked me to call him, received a copy of my book, *The Simple Truths of Appreciation - How Each of Us Can Make a Difference*, from his dear friend, Marlene. (You will read more about that story in the book.)

The first time he called me, he ordered 8 books to give to family and friends. He told me in that conversation that "he didn't have much time left and he wanted to make a difference." I was delighted to support and encourage him.

On his next call about two weeks later, he told me he was having so much fun giving the books away that he wanted to order 20 more. In that same conversation he told me he was 98 years old. Then he went on to tell me that he did email, he had an iPhone, he had his own website, and he even had a YouTube channel. I was enthralled - he is the most amazing role model of creative aging I have ever seen!

As he ordered more and more books and we talked again and again, I grew to love this wonderful man. One day I said to him, "Uncle Wayne, you should write a book about your life." He said he might do that if I helped him, so over the next several conversations,

I gave him some ideas and encouraged him to keep on with this project as a legacy to his extended family for many years to come.

When I received his final manuscript a few days ago, my heart was overflowing. As I told him, "You made me laugh. You made me cry. And you made me love you even more!"

However you are fortunate enough to receive a copy of this lovely book, you will be deeply touched by the venerable life of one of the kindest, most generous persons you will ever know. He is truly a model of our Lord Jesus Christ, though of course he has lived a whole lot longer and I think perhaps he has a better sense of humor! ;-) It is a privilege for me to write this preface for a precious man I deeply admire.

Barbara A. Glanz
CSP, SPAE, Hall of Fame Speaker

Preface

As I write this, I am sitting here in my living room, looking out at the peaceful Table Rock Lake. It is so relaxing to sit here and observe God's creation. I am reminded that God is in charge and I look forward to seeing him one day in Heaven.

I am ninety-nine years old, feeling good and I am on a roll. People ask me for my secret. My answer is: each morning when I start a new day, I have a choice. I can choose to be either happy or unhappy. Every day, I choose happy.

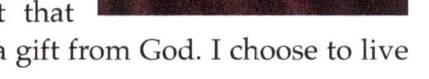

I have known sadness and grief, as this book will tell you. We cannot control what happens to us or around us, but we can control how we respond to what happens. Attitude is a choice. I choose how I live.

In addition, I look after my body by consuming a natural product that strengthens my body. My body is a gift from God. I choose to live healthily for God and for others.

I invite you to join me in the adventure of life, living spiritually and physically healthier.

I wrote this book to celebrate and share with you my life's journey, some of the many blessings I have enjoyed and lessons I have learned along the way. What God has done for me can also bless you.

What follows is a summary and blueprint of my life! Join me as I tell you my story and why I CHOOSE HAPPY!

Wayne Williams
January, 2020

Wayne and Rosie

Married in 1942

Table of Contents

Early Dust Bowl Days in the Texas and
  Oklahoma Panhandles..1
My Memories of Growing-up With
  My Parents..3
Three Happy Brothers: Bill, Don and Wayne..................6
Early Days with My Sister Bonnie (Sissy).......................10
How I Met and Married My Rosie..................................12
God's Precious Gifts to Us:
  Choosing Our Five Youngsters.....................................15
My Army Days (1944–1945)...26
My Early Days at Cessna Aircraft (1940–1959).............28
My Days of Home Building...30
Five Wonderful Years of Trips with Northside
  Church of Christ Young People (1971–1976)..............32
My Flying Days: Owning a Cessna 182
  (1978–1990)...34
How I Helped to Get Know Your Bible
  Up and Running in 1986..36
Church Growth in Shell Knob, Missouri:
  Bob and Marla Housby's Family (1993–1998)............39
Helping the Shell Knob Church to Build a
  New Building (1994)..41
Happy Days: Popo A.C. and Mom Margie....................43
My Days with a Health and Wellness Business:
  How it Has Improved My Health................................46

Meeting Quality People Like Ron and
  Marlene Brice in 2006...49
My life-saving Angel, Marlene, Showing
  Up in the Nick of Time..51
Goodbyes and Hellos...53
My Family Roots..55
Getting to Know My Family...58
"I Choose Happy!"...61
Sayings I Like..64
Thank You!..66
Wayne's Mission Statement And Philosophy
  For His Life On This Earth..68
"The Optimist"...70

I Choose Happy

Come, Join Me

Left to right: Bonnie Williams, Roseana Jane Page Williams, Errol Wayne Williams, Louis Tandy

Early Dust Bowl Days in the Texas and Oklahoma Panhandles

I was born into this world on May 21, 1920. When I was eleven years old in 1931, I first experienced total darkness from a huge Dust Bowl storm. I could not see my hand in front of my face. I had to put a wet towel over my nose and mouth in order to breathe. Those frequent Dust Bowl storms continued for years.

While in the seventh grade in Perryton, Texas, I met and became friends with Louis Tandy. In 1935 Louis and I were playing tennis at a local tennis court. We looked up from our game and saw dark, boiling clouds moving our way. Out came the wet towels for our faces as we immediately headed to our separate homes. Suddenly it was so dark that, once again, we could not see our hands in front of our faces.

In 1937 our family moved out of the Dust Bowl, from Perryton, Texas, to Wellington, Kansas. I WAS SO HAPPY to get away from those Dust Bowl days. But while living in Perryton I met and connected with a lot of people and made many close, treasured friends. Several years later my friend Louis moved to Wichita with his parents. He and I became best friends, and he was the best man at my wedding in 1942.

Wayne's Wisdom
What I have learned from life and others

> *Life is not always fun and sunshine. It can suddenly change and go dark, and the darkness can be overwhelming. But it never lasts. Light comes again. Trust God. He is always with us, and always stronger than the dark. We may not understand the work of his hands, but we can trust his heart!*
>
> *We need friends to share with us both joy and darkness. You can never have too many friends, so make them wherever you go. You never know when or how your friends may come back into your life, or how precious they may become to you.*

Wayne and his sister Bonnie

My Memories of Growing-up With My Parents

The Lord blessed me, as I was born into a preacher's family. My Dad was a minister of the Gospel. My Mom supported him as a stay-at-home wife and mother. She was a true helpmate and co-worker in their ministry. I had a solid, happy home life growing up because my folks gave me undying love. They also corrected me when I needed it, and for this I am grateful. I have the greatest respect for my parents who have gone on to be with the Lord.

My Dad was born May 20, 1897, and named Arthur Clyde Williams. Everyone knew him as "Brother A.C." He preached his first sermon at age seventeen in Bluejacket, Oklahoma. Many people responded to his first sermon. Later he met and married my mother, Mayme Melvina Kilpatrick, who was also born in 1897, before he went off to World War I. After the War, he came home and continued his preaching career. He also took classes, became qualified to be a public school teacher and worked at teaching, right along with his preaching. For ten years he was a teacher and, for part of this time, also a school principal. Then he became a full-time preacher.

I was their first child, born in 1920. A complication from delivery put my mother's life at risk and she hung between life and death for three months. My Aunt Stella saved me. She took me home with her and looked after me, day and night, for those three months.

During his preaching years, my father moved around from place to place, as he was needed. He would move to a town and get the church built up, then find another place that needed him. He began work as a minister in Canadian, Texas, in 1927 when I was seven. When I was in the first grade, we moved from Canadian, Texas, to Pomona, California, for Dad to serve there as a local minister. About two years later, Dad moved the family back to Oklahoma, to Greenough (near Forgan, in Beaver County), where he did local preaching work and was again a school teacher. The church building was just across the road from our house and the school building was about a mile down the road.

Sometime later, when I was in seventh grade, Dori Tandy asked my Dad to move to Perryton, Texas, to be their local minister. That is where I lived my Dust Bowl days and met my lifelong friend, Louis Tandy, who was my same age. From Perryton, we moved to Wellington, Kansas.

From Wellington, to Wichita, Kansas.

In Wichita, I married Rosie at the Cleveland Avenue Church of Christ on July 5, 1942.

Dad and Mom moved several other times. They moved to small congregations, built them up, then found someone that needed them more and moved there. From Wichita, to Winfield, Kansas. From Winfield, to Parsons, Kansas. From Parsons, to Sand Springs, Oklahoma. Richard was baptized in Sand Springs by my Dad while we were visiting them there.

From Sand Springs, they moved to Aurora, Missouri. From Aurora, they moved back to Wichita to retire. My Mom passed away in 1969 from cancer. Dad sold his home and came to live with Rosie and me in our home in north Wichita. My Dad stopped regular pulpit work at the age of eighty-five but was still teaching Bible class into his nineties. He left this earth at the age of ninety-seven in 1994.

Dad helped a lot of people in a lot of places as a preacher:

> Canadian, Texas (1927); Pomona, California (1928–29); Forgan, Oklahoma (1930–32); Perryton, Texas (1933–37); Wellington, Kansas (1937–41); Cleveland Ave. in Wichita, Kansas (1942-43); Poplar Ave. in Wichita, Kansas (1944–46); Winfield, Kansas (1947–1950); Parsons, Kansas (1950–53); Sand Springs, Oklahoma (1953–57); Aurora, Missouri (1957–1960).

My memories of growing up with Dad and Mom are of HAPPY, HAPPY DAYS.

Wayne's Wisdom

> *Honor your father and mother. If you have godly parents, be very grateful.*

Three Happy Brothers: Bill, Don and Wayne

I was born May 21, 1920. Don, my younger brother, was born October 7, 1925, and Bill (B'Gene), my youngest brother, was born June 5, 1927. What a delightful time I have had as I look back on growing up with my two younger brothers! Where do I begin with memories?

One first, vivid memory was when it came time for Dad to discipline us for something we did wrong. Out came the leather strap and Dad proceeded to spank our behinds. Popo's child-raising rule was, "Ignore what you can but, if there's a confrontation, you cannot afford to lose." B'Gene and I figured that out and we chose to let Popo win. We did not like the spankings, so we quickly took them and retreated, having received our punishments.

But not Don. He chose to use those times to pit Mom and Dad against each other. When his spankings began, he made a big ruckus and Dad proceeded to spank him harder. Soon Mom would call out to Dad, "Stop it, Clyde! You are gonna kill him!" He played Mom like a fiddle and it drove Dad to distraction, because both Don and Dad were very strong-willed.

Lesson learned by Wayne and B'Gene: settle down and the spanking will stop. Lesson learned by Don: keep up the ruckus and get help from your Mom. She'll say, "Clyde, quit your spanking! You're gonna kill him!" He, he

In 1934 when B'Gene was age seven, he told my Mom that he was tired of having to dry the dishes so often. "It is unfair," he said, "and I will just leave home." She said, "Okay, I'll help you pack." In her good nature, Mom helped him put a few things in a small suitcase and told him goodbye at the door. She sent him out to face the world. Secretly, she asked me to follow and keep an eye on him. I kept my distance for a while and, in a bit, there sat brother B'Gene on the curb, sobbing. I came to his rescue and together we walked back home. I do not remember how my Mom reacted, but I am certain it was with the kind, loving ways she had with all of us in all the years of growing up.

B'Gene reminded me of this next story. (You can't make this stuff up!) About 1941 B'Gene and I drove from Wichita, Kansas, to Chowchilla, California, for a family visit. He helped me to drive my Mercury convertible the 1500-plus miles, each way.

But for the return trip B'Gene was too sick to help, so he begged off and crawled into the back seat, leaving all the driving to me. We did not have money for motels so we drove all the way without stopping. About 4 a.m. we made it to a rest stop in Southwest Kansas. I had driven over 1,200 miles on two-lane highways and I was exhausted. B'Gene finally offered to help and I quickly handed him the keys, crawled into the backseat and was asleep before we ever left the rest stop.

B'Gene had not driven far when the sun came up. The Kansas highway had gravel shoulders that went off into wide bar ditches on each side, full of sunflowers. He tried to retrieve his sunglasses from the glove compartment while maintaining highway speed, took his eyes off the road for a moment and wandered onto the highway shoulder. As he started to correct, the front wheel dug into the

gravel and he realized that further correction risked rolling the convertible! So he decided instead to deliberately drive into the wide bar ditch. By the Lord's grace, he did not kill us both! He managed to get the car stopped without hitting anything in the ditch except for the sunflower plants that were in full bloom and taller than the car!

When we finally stopped, B'Gene turned around to see me. I had been abruptly awakened by the wild ride into the ditch and, as I sat up, all I could see in any direction were sunflowers! He said that he could not imagine what was going through my mind but he will never forget the look on my face!

We were able to drive the car back up onto the highway, and I decided to drive the rest of the way home to Wichita.

So many happy, happy memories of our time spent growing into adults. When I was in high school in Wellington, Kansas, I had scraped up enough money to buy an old clunker. Don and Bill, being younger, wanted to borrow it. While they were gone, Don contacted me and said he had experienced some trouble with the car. He had been driving along and the right front wheel came off. No crashes, but the car did not run very well on three wheels. We were able to make repairs and continue on, all of us growing up into adulthood.

Another precious time was at the balloon festival in Albuquerque where Don, Bill and I had a wonderful time. Here is a photo of the three of us there.

I celebrated my brother Don's ninetieth birthday party with him in Lubbock in 2015. Only a few months later I was back in Lubbock for his funeral to say goodbye. We lost Don April 10, 2016.

Such wonderful years, growing up with my brothers. I AM SO VERY, VERY HAPPY for all the delightful years we were able to spend together.

Wayne's Wisdom

> *How blessed we are when we have a family with which to share our lives!*

Early Days with My Sister Bonnie (Sissy)

Bonnie was born May 10, 1924, and passed away February 11, 1956.

I remember so many delightful fun times with my sister, Bonnie. She was four years younger than me and full of energy, spunk and surprises. I never knew what complete surprise she would come up with next.

As she grew older, it was so much fun just to sit and talk with her about anything and everything. Together we would make up jokes to pull on our two younger brothers, Don and Bill. They learned to expect the unexpected from us. As I look back on it now, I cherish the wonderful times I had just being in the presence of energy-driven Bonnie Lee, known to us all as Sissy.

Our Bonnie received a blood transfusion after a simple operation. This was in 1956, before testing blood for hepatitis was available. Tragically, Bonnie contracted hepatitis from which she never recovered. At the time, Bonnie was only thirty-one years old, a young mother living as a farmer's wife in St. John, Kansas, and blessed with four children: Lorraine, Jimmy, Vicki and Lana, ages 10, 7, 5, and 3 years.

Upon her passing, four little ones were left alone, to be cared for by her loving husband, Loyd. In the short time she had with her four youngsters, Bonnie made a lasting impression on each one. All four are now adults with hearts full of love and happiness.

The days I spent with Sissy Bonnie Lee were treasured days and I AM SO VERY, VERY HAPPY to have been a part of those wonderful memorable days.

Wayne's Wisdom

Time has no power over love. How long we live is not as important as how well we live. Each of us, like Bonnie, can make a lasting impact on the people in our life, even if our time with them is short.

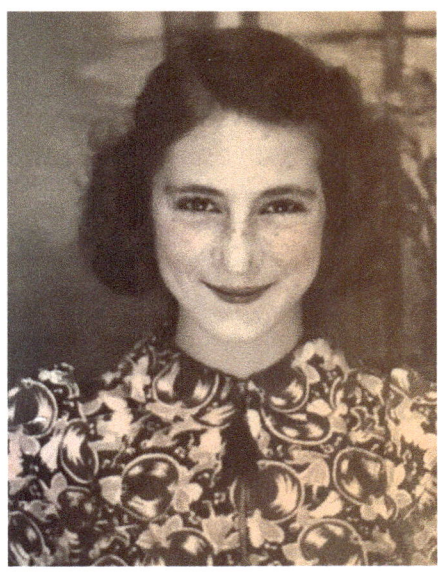

How I Met and Married My Rosie

I was fortunate to be a preacher's kid. One weekend, after my family moved to Wellington, Kansas, a young people's "Get Together" was scheduled at the church building. Young people groups from surrounding congregations were invited. Rosie, age fourteen, came to the meeting from the Emporia Avenue Church of Christ in Wichita.

I was seventeen when Rosie and I saw each other and connected. From the very first time I saw Rosie, I was a goner! I knew there would never be anyone else for me!

We kept in touch, but two years later Rosie's folks moved to California. I never forgot about Rosie. Back then, I spent a lot of money with Southwestern Bell Telephone Company, talking to Rosie. At the time, I was working at Cessna Aircraft.

In 1942 I persuaded Rosie to come back to Wichita. We were married July 5, 1942, and lived our lives together until four days short of seventy-two years. I do not have the right words to express HOW HAPPY I was during those seventy-two years.

I have always been a hugger. One day at church, a woman jokingly said to Rosie, "Do you know what Wayne is doing? He's out front, hugging all the girls!" Rosie said, "Oh, that's just the way Wayne is. I don't mind, as long as he doesn't start hugging just any one girl!"

Rosie passed away from a stroke June 29, 2014. During Rosie's funeral we celebrated her life and I spoke to her, over her casket. I said, "Rosie, I look forward to being with you again. Save me a seat!"

I also spoke to everyone gathered there and said, "On July 4th, 1942, Rosie and I celebrated Independence Day. The next day, on July 5th, we were married and blew that independence to smithereens—all away to the four winds!"

Wayne's Wisdom

> *Love is life's greatest gift, and death cannot defeat love. Death may keep us from those we love for a while, but we are sustained by the hope that someday we will see them again, after this life is over.*

Taken on day of Rosie's funeral. Wayne sits between Yvonne Williams (Don's widow) and Bill (B'Gene), his brother.

God's Precious Gifts to Us: Choosing Our Five Youngsters

Not flesh of my flesh
Nor bone of my bone,
But still miraculously my own.
Never forget for a single minute,
You didn't grow under my heart,
But in it.
—*Fleur Conkling Heyliger*

Shortly after we were married, my Rosie suffered a critical physical condition which required an operation to save her life. After the operation, she could not have children. We discussed this and, by mutual consent, we decided to go the route of adoption. Time rolled around and we legally adopted four children: Richard, Pennie, Bobby and Polly. When my sister Bonnie died, we added to our family her three-year-old daughter, Lana, who was deaf.

I was busy making a living as a custom home builder and the lion's share of raising these youngsters fell to Rosie. I am so grateful for the effort and love that Rosie poured into their young lives. Being a part of changing these lives has been such a blessing for me and I AM SO HAPPY to have been a part of their lives.

Let me tell you about each of them, and how they came to us.

My Son Richard

Richard was our first adopted child.

One day when Richard was six years old, he came home with a friend, crying his eyes out. Rosie asked him why he was crying so hard. He said, "My friend is making fun of me because I am adopted." Rosie gently said to Richard, "Your Dad and Mom picked you out. You were selected! You tell your little friend here that his parents had to take him, whether they wanted to or not!" The little guy started crying and ran home. Soon his momma called Rosie   and was complaining. Rosie said to the little boy's momma, "YOU SHOULD HAVE KEPT YOUR MOUTH SHUT!"

 When he was seven years old, Richard was infected with spinal meningitis. His nurses and doctors showed him much love and care and he fully recovered. I remember him saying on the way home from the hospital, "When I grow

> May 31, 1970
>
> Dear Mom and Dad:
>
> This month we reach together what all of us have been working toward for the last 25 years. I am about to become self-supporting. I say we together, for without you, I wouldn't be the things I am. You are both always telling me how proud you are of me. I appreciate that, but it's not me we all should be proud of, it's both of you. If it hadn't been for you, Mom, I wouldn't have the determination and spirit to be granted an M.D. If not for you, Dad, I wouldn't have the deep sense of gratitude, self-reliance, and sense of fairness it takes to be a physician. If not for the both of you I wouldn't be the Christian adult I am today.
>
> This letter is not intended to be boastful, for I have accomplished more than I had ever hoped, but I owe the better part of it all to two people that started me in life, gave me my initiative, and stood behind me in all manner of adversity. You permitted me my independence when I needed it yet always allowed me the security to call upon you, also, when needed. It's beyond me to tell you of the gratitude I feel for you both. I can only offer that when I walk down the hill to receive my M.D. degree, it's not just me but all of us together that will be receiving it.
>
> Thank you both for the person I am.
>
> With much Love,
>
> *Richard*

up, I want to be a doctor and help others like I was helped." He never took his eyes off that lifetime goal. First impressions are powerful.

With unwavering support from Beverly, the love of his life, Richard spent four years at Abilene Christian College in Abilene, Texas. Next he spent four years of medical school at Kansas University Medical School in Kansas City. Following that, he had two years of General Surgery Residency and five years of Urology Residency at the University of Minnesota in Minneapolis. It took fifteen years of training for him to become a Board-Certified Urologist—a medical plumber who goes about saving countless lives. My life was in building homes and in a good-natured way I said to Richard, "I can train plumbers quicker than fifteen years." He, he.

Richard was not tall. One day, Ann Tandy asked him why he chose to be a urologist. Richard's quick answer was, "Well, Mrs. Tandy. I'm short! That is as high as I can reach." What made this so comical is that Ann asked him this while several church ladies were listening. Her reaction was hilarious.

I AM SO HAPPY to have watched Richard's life unfold. Lung cancer claimed his life on May 28, 2010. He had served over thirty-four years as a urologist. He was Professor and Head of the Department of Urology at the University of Iowa for twenty-six years. Among his many awards, in 2005 he received the International Volunteers in Urology Award for Mentor of the Year for the twenty-plus years he volunteered, bringing residents and nurses with him to provide urologic care to the people of Haiti. Another cherished honor Richard received was the Hugh Hampton Young Award. Each year the American Urological Association awards this to just one urologist in the nation.  Richard was honored with this award in 2009 for outstanding contribution to Urologic Oncology, especially prostate cancer, and for tireless devotion to physician and patient education. I was present when the Dean of the University of Iowa Hospitals and Clinics came to his home to tell him that they were honoring Richard by naming his favorite operating room after him and that they would place a plaque in his honor next to it. This was the first named OR at the University, and it was a State-approved change. They also named the main operating suite after him.

Richard and Beverly asked Rosie and me to come to the Lake of the Ozarks for a weekend. During lunch at his favorite restaurant he shared with us what he told the room of doctors as he accepted this last award. He said to them that all of his close friends know that he was adopted, but he wanted all of those present to know how much he wanted to thank Rosie and me for adopting him and caring for him. He gave us credit for raising him and supporting him and said that he knew that all of his awards would not have been possible without our loving care.

Richard and Beverly had one child, Wendy Ellis, a true delight, who has helped me in so many ways over the years. Wendy is married to Geoff Ellis and they have two children, Kenzie, who lives in Tulsa and helps underprivileged children, and Tate, who is a student at the University of Colorado. Two great-grandchildren!

I am so proud of my son, Richard, and what he accomplished at the top of the medical world.

While I was creating this book, I needed a procedure done by Dr. David Anderson in Springfield, Missouri. After he completed his initial examination, he pulled me aside and said, "I trained under your son, Richard, for six years." Richard is gone, but his influence for good continues. His students know what to do, and one just took care of me! How about that!

My Daughter Pennie

My Rosie spent many selfless hours fixing hair for young girls at the Maude Carpenter Children's Home in Wichita. (My niece, Karen Juarez, told me years later that she has many pleasant memories of Rosie fixing her and her sister's hair on a regular basis. That made an impression on Karen.)

One cute twelve-year-old at Maude Carpenters named Pennie connected with Rosie in a special way. We decided by mutual consent to bring Pennie into our home as a foster child, because her mother would not allow adoption. When she turned sixteen, Pennie was old enough to give her consent and we were able to adopt her.

When Pennie was fourteen, we were in a terrible car crash while we were on the way to see my parents in Missouri. A young man driving another car went to sleep and hit us head-on. Pennie took most of the impact of the crumpled door post and she had to have major reconstructive surgery. She is a fighter and she made a full recovery. Today she is beautiful, and I AM SO HAPPY and proud of Pennie.

I asked Pennie about memories that stuck in her mind as she was growing up in our home. She said that, when she was sixteen, she had just received her student driver's permit. Her mother asked her to go and back the car out of the garage. This was new to her. She managed to scrape the right side of the car and it made an awful sound. She went inside and told her mom about it. Instead of getting upset, Rosie laughed and told her if that was the worst thing she ever did, not to worry. She remembered hearing Rosie also saying, "You should have been here when Richard pulled some of his tricks!" Pennie never forgot the kind way her mom reacted to her first major auto incident.

Pennie worked for twenty-five years with Walmart and was sunshine and a favorite to many there. She supervised the jewelry department until an accident with a slick floor took her off that job.

After some healing Pennie went back to work, but in early 2019 she retired and now lives in Goddard, Kansas. Her oldest son, Scott Perry, and his wife, Tamara, live in Choctaw, Oklahoma, and have given me two great-granddaughters, Brie and Emily. Her son, Jason Kennedy, lives next door to her and works with a company that builds cabinets for airplanes. Pennie's daughter, Amber Medrano, and her husband, Johnnie, live in Lubbock, Texas, and have blessed me with two great-granddaughters named Brenna and Bella.

I am so proud of Pennie for her zest for life, her determination, her humor, her faith in God and her passion for caring for others. Pennie is incredibly creative and is also an accomplished writer of poems. I have encouraged her to publish them.

My Niece Lana

In 1956 hepatitis took the life of my beautiful sister, Bonnie, at the age of 31. Their three-year-old daughter, Lana, who was born deaf, would need special training to help her communicate with the world.

Rosie asked if we could have a hand in helping Lana and I, of course, agreed. Rosie poured her life of love into helping Lana to get through her growing-up years—so many struggles with being deaf and learning to connect with the world.

Bonnie's oldest child, Lorraine Brock, is six years older than Lana and watched her grow up. She says: "Lana is one of the most AMAZING people I have ever known! From the very beginning, against so many odds, as a child born without the ability to hear with her own ears, Lana has always displayed a unique awareness to her environment, curiosity and willingness to learn. Early in life, Lana learned to read with her eyes and rely on observations for so much information, studying the feelings and emotions of people around her.

"With tireless and loving support from Aunt Rosie, Lana learned to be an excellent lip reader. She became an expert at reading faces, catching words and following conversations.

"Lana was always interested in learning and thrilled to understand anything. She was always asking me to explain words that she picked up in sermons and classes at church. She wanted to understand the language she heard and she would always ask me, 'What does that mean?'"

Lana attended York College in Nebraska and Oklahoma Christian College in Oklahoma. At OCC, she decided to learn American Sign Language (ASL) so that she could teach the Bible to deaf children. Lorraine said, "I will NEVER FORGET how thrilled Lana was when she told me how learning to use sign language had totally changed her understanding of the Bible—from 'black and white' to 'COLOR'! That said so much about her gratitude for learning to sign!"

So many happy hours we spent helping Lana to grow into a happy adult! She lived with us until age twenty. In 1976 Lana found her soulmate in a young deaf man named Steve Farmer and they were married in 1978. Today they live happily in Chattanooga, Tennessee. Lorraine says it best: "Lana and Steve have been pillars in their Christian community for decades by being able to teach and communicate so well, using both languages—spoken English and ASL—with gentleness and love. Lana possesses a unique and incredible ability to communicate with both hearing and deaf—and often at the same time! Lana is as kind and genuinely loving a soul as you can find. Her devotion to God and others is inspiring. She has always been 'wise beyond her years.' I want to be like Lana when I grow up!"

I AM SO HAPPY to have been a part of Lana's life and to watch her grow up.

My Son Bobby

In 1960 Rosie learned about a baby whose mother was unable to keep him. Of course, we decided to give this baby a solid home and completed the process to do so, taking him into our home directly from the hospital.

What a delightful, happy time we experienced in helping him grow into a happy adult.

Bobby faced many challenges in life as we helped him to grow into adulthood. In 1987 he met Diane Newcomb. They were married on September 30, 1988. To this union a daughter named Amy Williams was born.

Amy shared with me this memory of Bobby: "During Christmas weekend of 1993, the best printing press in Branson had their annual Christmas holiday party. My dad had been working there for about six months. Mom and Dad put on their best and headed to the celebration! Dinner was delicious, the company delightful and fun was had by all. As the party came to a close, Dad was presented with a very special award: Employee of the Year. In all of its years, the company had never given this award before!! Dad had worked so hard at that job and always put his best foot forward, so this was an incredible honor and well-deserved!!"

On Valentine's Day 1995, Bobby was tragically killed in an auto accident. At the time, Bobby and Diane were managers for me at a business known as Storage Village in Branson West, Missouri. This was a mini storage warehouse facility of 350 units. Diane and her young family moved to Las Cruces, New Mexico, and I sold that facility.

Amy is a beautiful young lady and works in the business world. I AM SO HAPPY that we were able to give our Bobby a solid home as he grew into adulthood.

My Daughter Polly

Polly was six-and-a-half-years-old when she joined our family. We met and fell in love with Polly while she was in foster care with my brother Don and his wife, Von. During family visits Polly would often follow Rosie around and they developed a unique and very special connection. It became obvious that they had captured each other's hearts. Rosie asked me if we could adopt Polly and, of course, I agreed.

What wonderful years we experienced watching and helping Polly grow up into a beautiful young lady. I AM SO HAPPY to have helped and watched Polly grow.

I asked Polly what she remembered that was unforgettable about her growing up years. She recalled a very special 16th birthday party. She also remembered her water-skiing days. In her teens, she was excellent at riding on one ski and I pulled her all over the lake. Polly was unstoppable! She figured out how to put the ski rope around her waist and go another thirty miles. The only way I could get her off the skis was to shut down the boat!

I am so proud of Polly. Her loving nature and huge, giving heart has been evident throughout her life in her personal and church family relationships. She loves deeply. She loves to give love and share love. For the last several years, Polly has used her compassion and giving spirit in her work as a paraprofessional supporting special needs children on their way to and from school.

Polly and Noel Shortt were married August 11, 1980. Their dedication to God and service to others throughout their marriage is evident and encouraging to all who know them. To this union were born two daughters, Linda and Noella. Linda Anguiano is married to John and they have blessed me with three great-grandsons named Dominic, Roman and Elias. Noella has two more of my great-grandsons and they are named Kamerynn and Khryztian.

I am so pleased that Rosie and I could be a part of Polly's life, as she has grown into a beautiful Christian woman—a mother, a grandmother and someone with a huge, wonderful heart full of love.

Wayne's Wisdom

> *The Lord moves in mysterious ways. If Rosie had been able to give birth, these five beautiful children would not have come into our lives as they did. The Lord turned our sadness into joy! I cannot imagine what my life, or theirs, would be like today if that had not happened!*
>
> *Give of yourself, invest in other people, and you will never be sorry.*

Lana, Wayne, Bobby, Rosie, Polly, Pennie

My Army Days
(1944–1945)

In 1943 I was working at Cessna Aircraft and decided to enlist in the Army Air Corp to become a pilot. The Army Air Corp name was changed later to Army Air Force. My enlistment began on April 13, 1944, and I moved from Manhattan, Kansas, to basic training in Amarillo, Texas, then to Victorville, California. I was tested for all the skills needed to fly a plane, passed them all with flying colors and was ready to start my flying career.

I was scheduled to ship out the next week to flying school when President Harry Truman decided to drop the atomic bombs on Hiroshima and Nagasaki, Japan. That promptly ended World War II.

Now suddenly all of us flying cadets were named "On the Line Trainees." Every kind of job was given to us. I was given a 200-pound jackhammer to break up concrete. Since I weighed only 125 pounds at the time, I complained. I had photo experience, so I was then given a job as an aerial photographer, flying around in a B-24, doing aerial mapping. Truth of the matter was that all of us who were ready for flying school were excess soldiers. The Air Force was in the process of separating us from the service. No flying school anymore. The War was over.

For some reason, I was sent to Biloxi, Mississippi, then transferred to Travis Field in California, then sent to Milwaukee, Wisconsin, and discharged on November 25, 1945. All of this experience in the Air Force was a very interesting time in my life, to say the least.

I WAS SO HAPPY TO COME HOME and be with my soulmate, Rosie, and our little feisty Richard.

Wayne's Wisdom

> *Serve however you can, bloom where you are planted and learn to adjust. "Blessed are the flexible, for they shall not be broken." When you get to be my age, if you're not able to adjust, you might as well hang it up!*

My Early Days at Cessna Aircraft (1940–1959)

I went to work at Cessna in 1940, at the pay rate of forty cents per hour. As a young single man, twenty years of age, I was able to do just fine, financially. I was on a learning curve and daily increasing my knowledge of how to schedule production assembly lines. This knowledge and experience allowed me to get promoted to Supervisor of Production Line Scheduling. At this time, we were building forty airplanes per month. The model we were building was the Cessna 140, the first of their many successful models.

I married my Rosie in 1942 and late 1943 enlisted in the Army Air Corps. A year later, on August 14, 1945, the War ended and I soon came home. Cessna had held my job open and I picked up where I left off.

I continued with Cessna for fifteen years and during that time I was able to use my GI Bill to get my private flying license. As a Cessna supervisor and with a current private license, I was qualified to deliver new planes to new places like New Orleans and Oakland, California. This allowed me to increase my flying hours.

I ENJOYED HAPPY DAYS INDEED AT CESSNA.

In 1959 a friend offered to teach me the home building business. With the full support of Rosie, I left Cessna and began my new life of building homes. The next chapter tells of my custom home building journey.

Wayne's Wisdom

Life is a journey, not a destination. Enjoy every chapter life brings you! And always keep your eyes open for new possibilities and opportunities.

My Days of Home Building

In 1959 I made the decision to leave Cessna Aircraft and move out into a new world—a world of learning the construction business. I began by building tract homes. What a challenge!

At Cessna, I had been in a protected environment—inside, with no weather problems. I got a shock when I found myself rising from my sleep and going out in the raw elements of rain, snow and ice.

To be able to satisfy Wichita home building inspectors, I had to take a test in the City Hall to become a bona fide home builder. This required me to quickly learn the skills needed in order to answer the test questions. I studied, did my homework and was able to complete the test and obtain a valid home builder license. What a relief!

My friend, Don Mundell, who had encouraged me to leave Cessna, was proud of my accomplishment. I went on in my building career until 1990, when we moved to my cabin and landing strip in Shell Knob, Missouri. I have lived here, full-time, since that move.

At this writing, the year is 2019. During my building career, from 1959 to 1990—some 31 years—I faced many challenges. In addition to homes, I took on apartment buildings, church buildings and commercial buildings, like a 711-unit building in Rose Hill, Kansas, in 1986. Each new undertaking was a different challenge, all its own.

In Shell Knob, my philosophy of giving full service caught up with me. Some people I had built homes for in Wichita also bought vacant lots here on the Lake. When the word got out that I was retired and living in this area, I was approached by various past customers who asked if I would help them with their building projects. I took a different path this time. I helped them, but only as a project manager, with them paying the bills. No more firm contracts to build a home. After three or four years of this, my Rosie talked directly to me and said in kind words, "I thought you were coming here to retire. I am tired of you waking me up at 5:30 in the morning, arguing with concrete companies." My son, Richard, got into the conversation and, between Rosie and Richard, I was persuaded to stop helping people to build homes.

About this time, a new Shell Knob church building was needed. In another chapter, I will tell how I was able to save the church a lot of money.

I AM SO HAPPY TO HAVE HAD THE EXPERIENCE of building homes, apartments, office buildings, and church buildings for 31 years before moving to the Lake in 1990.

Wayne's Wisdom

One thing that my dad told me that I always remembered: "In this life you will need to make promises to people. Do whatever you need to do to keep those promises—I don't care if it costs you $3000!"

All my success as a builder came because I was a straight arrow. I gave people full measure of my effort. Besides, I wasn't smart enough to cheat people, even if I had wanted to! Give full service to everyone you work for and your work will always be valued and needed.

And when it is time to rest, stop and rest.

Five Wonderful Years of Trips with Northside Church of Christ Young People (1971–1976)

As our children were growing up, Rosie and I chose to expand their experiences and help them to grow closer to the Lord. Each February of the traveling years, we rounded up interested young people from the Northside Church of Christ and gave them special training focused on learning how to conduct a Vacation Bible School.

We found out-of-state congregations that needed a Vacation Bible School and scheduled bus trips to those locations. BIG LOUIE, our church bus, took our group to places like Sundae, Wyoming; Minot, North Dakota; Albuquerque, New Mexico; Raton, Nevada; and more.

We would gather together a group of some thirty youngsters ready to make the trip and all the materials needed for the Vacation Bible School. Since the trips were rather long, we found church buildings along the way where we could stop and house the youngsters for the night, with the girls in one section and the boys in another. Most of the church buildings had basements. At one church, the girls got to talking and some wanted to be baptized right then. The baptistry was ready, so I baptized several girls that night in some of the coldest water I have ever been in! I am still shivering!

A highlight of these trips was the one we made to Albuquerque, New Mexico. Rosie and I had thirty young people on our bus. We drove them up into the mountains and conducted a Vacation

Bible School at Sandia Camp for thirty young people from Mission Albuquerque, an intercity mission program. Our nephew, Gary Williams, and other local Christians who led that ministry joined us. We assigned an intercity youngster to each of our young people and told our workers that they had to look after that young person for a week. Then we took the young people on an exciting tram trip to the top of the Sandia Mountains.

Many people helped us to create these trips. They included Eleanor Peterson, Jim and Irene Ford, Lindy Heins, and Dean and Diane Nelsen. My life was enriched as we travelled together, all over, for five years. I AM SO HAPPY TO HAVE BEEN ABLE TO SHARE THESE DAYS WITH THESE OUTSTANDING YOUNG PEOPLE.

Wayne's Wisdom

Life is teamwork, like building a house. Someone needs to pour the foundation. You need an excavator, and also someone to do the drywall. You've got to have framers and electricians. And don't forget the plumbing! It takes many people, working together, to succeed.

What you invest in young people is an investment in the future, especially when you teach them about Jesus.

My Flying Days: Owning a Cessna 182
(1978–1990)

I had a valid flying license but I was inactive with flying. In 1978 Larry Rahal visited me at my office. Larry was a test pilot for Cessna Aircraft and a Certified Flight Instructor. While we were talking, he learned of my interest in flying and asked me a very important question: did I want to go back to flying? This peaked my interest.

Together we went airplane shopping, found a 1964 Cessna 182 and bought it. Larry gave me brush-up lessons and signed my log book so I could legally fly this recently-purchased Cessna 182.

I was building homes in Wichita and had recently bought eighty acres on the lake in Shell Knob, Missouri. This property had a grass landing strip on it and it worked out just fine for me to land the Cessna 182 there. The landing strip is 5700 feet long, with trees at both ends. For twelve years, I made the trip, flying from Wichita to Shell Knob, almost every weekend.

At this writing, I am living in the little cabin that came with that land purchase. During those twelve years, I flew my family all over the United States—cities such as New Orleans; San Francisco; Chattanooga; Tulsa; Albuquerque; York, Nebraska and many more.

Rosie did not like riding in this airplane because she did not know how to land it in an emergency, so I asked her if she wanted to take lessons. This she did, and she went ahead and soloed. She felt more comfortable and was a better copilot from that time forward.

Those twelve years of flying (over 800 hours) were some of the most HAPPY, HAPPY, HAPPY times of my life. I looked it up. The Cessna 182 (identified as 1836 X Ray) is still flying somewhere in Texas.

I have not been at the controls of any airplane for twenty-eight years. Anyone want to go with me on a check ride? He, he

Wayne's Wisdom

> *Travel is a precious gift! Do as much of it as you can! And wherever you go, look for ways to connect with people, have fun and lighten their day. If you can't have fun with what you do, just stay home! Whenever I board an airplane, I say to the pilots, "I've got 800 hours in a Cessna 182! Want some help?" I have many great conversations and make new friends that way.*

Left: Wayne Williams and Ron Brice

How I Helped to Get Know Your Bible Up and Running in 1986

The Lord blessed my life and led me to enjoy twenty years in a leadership role as one of the elders of the Northside Church of Christ.

In 1981 I made a trip to San Diego, California, to see about a business deal. A potential customer wanted to build some apartments in Wichita and he wanted me to see what he had in mind. While there, I stayed in the home of my Uncle Ross and Aunt Mildred and went to church with them one Sunday morning. Uncle Ross was excited to show me a TV program that they were sponsoring named KNOW YOUR BIBLE. Uncle Ross recorded it, on one of the old VCR formats, and I brought the tape back to Wichita.

I showed it to the elders and congregation of the Northside Side Church of Christ and asked for their feedback. Was there any interest in us taking on a program like this? The elders and the congregation were enthused and wanted to start it right away. I started calling local TV stations but found out that all of their times for programs like this were already spoken for. But I did not want to give up.

My executive secretary, Marlys McFerren, faithfully reminded me on a regular basis to call the TV stations. I made those calls, and this went on for five years, from 1981 to 1986. Without her reminders, I probably would have let the opportunity slip by.

One day in 1986, I was leaving for a business trip to Chicago and would have been out the door in ten minutes when Marlys stopped me and said, "I think you need to take this call before you leave." I heard a voice on the phone say, "Wayne, you have been bugging me for a long, long time to air your program. A spot has come open for 10:00 am on Sunday mornings. This is Thursday, and I need to know if you want it by a week from tomorrow—next Friday." I had eight days to give them an answer. I asked him the cost. He said, "Once a week for one year for $60,000, or a six-month commitment for $30,000." I called one of the elders, Marvin Casebolt, and explained the situation. I told him I would be back in town Saturday afternoon and asked if he would round up the men of the congregation for a meeting.

The amount of money shocked and frightened some of the men. Then our minister, Steve Tandy (the son of my old friend, Louis Tandy), asked this question: "Could it just be that the Lord is testing us, to see our reaction? For five years we have been trying to get a time for this show. Now we have one, and the question is: what are we going to do?" Four of us elders talked it over and decided to go ahead with the program. The next Monday we met at the station and all four of us, individually, signed the contract for one year.

Now the story gets interesting.

The program began, and now we had to find the money to pay for it. We took this to the congregation and said, "In a couple of weeks, we are going to have a special collection to meet our costs for the program." That Sunday we had the regular collection and then, at the end of the service, it was time for the KNOW YOUR BIBLE collection. I was shocked when the amount was totaled: $52,000.00! The regular weekly contribution did not decrease. The Lord's hand was in this, for sure.

Steve Tandy recently sent me a note to say that they had just completed 1400 programs. Can you imagine the number of hours of study and time it has taken to record and broadcast 1400 different programs over thirty-four years?

The other day in Shell Knob, I sat behind a woman at church who I did not know. She told me that her name is Paulette Ward, that she is a member of the Northside Church of Christ in Wichita and that for thirty years she has answered the phone for Know Your Bible and graded the correspondence courses it offers.

I AM SO HAPPY TO HAVE BEEN A PART OF HELPING TO GET THE KNOW YOUR BIBLE PROGRAM UP AND GOING. Thirty-four years of sowing the seeds of the kingdom and changing lives for hundreds of people!

Wayne's Wisdom

If you believe that God wants you to do something, keep knocking at the door with patience and persistence. If God is in it, he will open the door for you.

To learn about Know Your Bible, go to:
www.knowyourbible.com.

Church Growth in Shell Knob, Missouri: Bob and Marla Housby's Family (1993–1998)

In 1993 Ben Loudermilk, the regular minister at our local Shell Knob Church of Christ, announced that he was retiring. He told us that he had talked to Marla Housby and learned that her husband was searching for a place to preach. At that time Bob, Marla and their son, Jason, were living in Abilene, Texas. The men of the congregation agreed that a trip to Abilene to talk to Bob and his family was in order, so Don Williams and I made the journey there and visited them. This resulted in Bob and his family making the move to Shell Knob.

Bob and Marla joined the Shell Knob Church family and went to work preaching, visiting families and building up the congregation. When Bob and Marla began in 1993, there were twenty-five or thirty people attending. After five years, the congregation had grown to about eighty. I credit this church growth to the personal work that Bob and Marla were able to accomplish. Many other hands helped achieve this growth.

When I look back over this time, I AM SO VERY, VERY HAPPY that I was able to watch this church grow during 1993 to 1998. Their son, Jason Housby, was in the fourth grade when they moved to Shell Knob. Today after all these years, Jason is a successful IT technician and lives in Des Moines, Iowa. He owns HCS: Housby Consulting Services (jason@housbycs.com). Bob and Marla remain in fulltime ministry, including Italian Missions.

Wayne's Wisdom

Remember when I said you never know when and how friends may come back into your life? Young Jason Housby has become a close friend who has helped me to create this book!

Matt, Erline, Barbara, Bud, Wayne

Helping the Shell Knob Church to Build a New Building
(1994)

In 1994 a church fire in the middle of the night caused the destruction of the long-standing building known as the Shell Knob Church of Christ. Temporary arrangements were made for immediate use of a small, available building facility known as a laundromat. While these temporary facilities were used each Sunday, the church's future plans were up in the air.

Olen Epperly had five acres of land nearby and offered this ground to the church at a very generous discount. We paid $8000.00 for five acres which had a value of $30,000.00 on the open market.

Three years before I moved to Shell Knob, while building homes and church buildings full-time, I worked on a set of church plans for a small congregation in the town of Belle Plaine, south of Wichita. Shortly before I left Wichita,  this church building project came to a stop because the elders suddenly passed away. I had made an investment in these church plans and brought them with me to Shell Knob. I offered these to the Shell Knob church, free of charge.

Some of the men of the church were doubtful we could afford to use this set of plans but, on faith, we started the building process. I told the subcontractors that we did not have any funds, but I would guarantee that, as money came in, they would be paid. I personally guaranteed it.

The Lord's hand was in this building project from the start. As work was completed and bills were presented, money showed up to pay the bills. This continued throughout the entire building project. When it was finished, a short loan of $3000.00 came in from outside sources and paid off the remaining costs. This let us have a newly-constructed church building, with no debt. In addition, a Kansas City church was remodeling and it delivered to us—free of any costs to us—a complete set of pews.

End of construction story. Today the building is used for services and it is free of any debt. This building, along with the five acres, has an estimated value of some $750,000.

I AM SO HAPPY to have been a part of this construction project.

Wayne's Wisdom

No part of your life is wasted. You never know how something you did or learned years ago may enable you to help someone tomorrow.

Happy Days: Popo A.C. and Mom Margie

While Dad was living with us on 37th Street in Wichita, Kansas, he became interested in a "young lady" in Tulsa, Oklahoma. I noticed that he was getting on the bus and taking trips to Tulsa, then returning a few days later to Wichita. On one such trip, he never returned. It turned out he was in love with Marjorie Millikan, a woman he had known for over sixty years. Their friendship began in the 1920s. Marjorie was one of his students when he was a young teacher in the Oklahoma Panhandle, and she was there when he preached his first sermon. They loved telling this story. Both had survived their spouses and had three sons. As they each married and started families, they remained close friends. He officiated at the weddings of two of her sons. When each became widowed, the other was there to lean on. "We've been friends forever," they said. "We've seen a lot of years and a lot of people come and go."

They decided to get married in Tulsa, Oklahoma, on January 1, 1982. Mom Margie's sons were named Arlen, Gary and Jack. Popo's sons were named Wayne, Don and Bill. My little brother Don served as the marrying minister and all of us boys, on both sides of the union, stood up with them as they were married. Of course, Dad then left Rosie and me and moved to Mom Margie's house in Tulsa.

Marjorie and great-great-granddaughter Tamarra Brock, great-granddaughter of Bonnie

This was a marriage made in Heaven, and we watched in admiration as they spent their twilight years together. They were as happy as any young couple could ever be.

While Popo lived with Rosie and me, he grew a huge garden and took trunk loads of its fruits to church and let everyone come and pick up what they wanted. Again, after he moved to Tulsa, he and Mom Margie grew a huge garden in their backyard, and the neighbors and church people received a large portion of its generous bounty.

Eighty years after he preached his first sermon in Bluejacket, Oklahoma, at age seventeen, Popo passed away August 25, 1994, at the age of ninety-seven. That is eighty years of preaching the gospel, bringing people to the Lord and changing lives. His passion to keep learning and studying never stopped. While he lived in our home, I would go by his bedroom door in the middle of the night and hear his typewriter going clicky, clicky, clicky. He was putting down on paper his thoughts and writing his wonderful poems.

Here are the opening lines of one of his poems, titled *I Walked the Path of Suffering*:

> I walked the path of suffering—I thought I was alone.
> But soon I found that others had heartaches like my own
> A legion came to join me—an understanding throng,
> To share and bear my burdens—heal suffering with song.

I AM SO HAPPY that I got to watch the happy days of Mom Margie and Popo in their twilight years. When they married, Popo was eighty-four and Marjorie was seventy-four, and they still had almost thirteen years together!

Wayne's Wisdom

Happiness knows no age. It is never too late to find it.

Popo AC, age 85, playing banjo in his home in Tulsa, OK

Xango Rush 2015

My Days with a Health and Wellness Business: How it Has Improved My Health

The next chapter in this book tells about my brother Bill and Don inviting me to a meeting that Ron and Marlene Brice were putting on in Branson, Missouri, in 2006. That meeting turned out to be a life-changer for me. I was introduced to a natural fruit drink based on mangosteen, a tropical fruit native to Southeast Asia. I have consumed a bottle of this juice drink every week since 2006. I take it three times a day with my meals. Before being introduced to this product, I was forever getting sick, getting the flu every winter, had flaky hair and I have type 2 diabetes that was not well-controlled.

I have not been sick since 2006—with the exception of my self-induced overdose of insulin, explained in another chapter. Before I was introduced to mangosteen, my A1C test results were off the charts—regularly showing levels of 12 or 13. I started consuming this mangosteen drink and now my A1C tests results come in at a level of 7.0. I have more energy. I have not been sick, have no flaky hair and have more energy.

The next two chapters tell how life-changing it has been for me to meet up with Ron and Marlene and the mangosteen fruit juice.

I AM SO VERY HAPPY the Lord has arranged for me to consume mangosteen on a regular basis.

Wayne's Wisdom

> *Take care of your body. If you don't have your health, you don't have diddly-squat!*

Sherman Unkefer and Wayne Williams

Wayne Williams and Ray Herron

Chris Estes, Wayne Williams and Dwayne Dyer

Jason Housby, Karl Anderson and Wayne Williams

Richard O'Brien, Karol O'Brien, Dwayne Dyer, and Wayne Williams

Kent Wood, Wayne Williams, and Gordon Morton

Gordon Morton, Sr. and Wayne Williams

Jason Housby, Beverly Hollister, and Wayne Williams

Meeting Quality People Like Ron and Marlene Brice in 2006

My journey of finding the health and wealth business way of life has been such a delightful blessing to my life. Meeting one special couple was life-changing for me. I was introduced to them in the fall of 2006 at a special meeting they engineered at the Chateau on the Lake Convention Center in Branson, Missouri. I was invited to this meeting by my brother, Bill, who was living in Albuquerque, New Mexico, at the time. I live in Shell Knob, Missouri, just across the lake from Branson.

I want you to realize how important first impressions are. The impression Ron and Marlene made on me at this meeting was transformative. Their high-quality, professional presentations were truly impressive. I quickly developed a close and lasting friendship with them.

Sadly, we lost Ron in 2012, but I have been blessed with a continued close friendship with Marlene. She is the lifesaving angel that the next chapter in this book talks about. You can see her photo in that chapter.

This health and wellness business has been such a positive part of my life. Not only has consuming these natural products extended my life but it has made it possible for me to meet and develop friendships with many very successful people. I would never have had this opportunity without first getting to know Ron and Marlene Brice.

I AM SO HAPPY the Lord arranged for me to meet these wonderful people.

Wayne's Wisdom

Find good friends and cherish them. We become what we are because of the books we read and the friends we make. As the Bible says,

**You use steel to sharpen steel,
and one friend sharpens another.
—Proverbs 27:17 (MSG)**

Ron & Marlene Brice, Rosie & Wayne Williams

My life-saving Angel, Marlene, Showing Up in the Nick of Time

I would not be writing this book except for the fast action of my life-saving Angel named Marlene. In January, 2017, I woke up one morning and, before taking my blood sugar reading for my type 2 diabetes, I took an extra insulin shot. My blood sugar was too low, and that affected my mind. I overdosed with too much insulin. I walked into the living room and passed out.

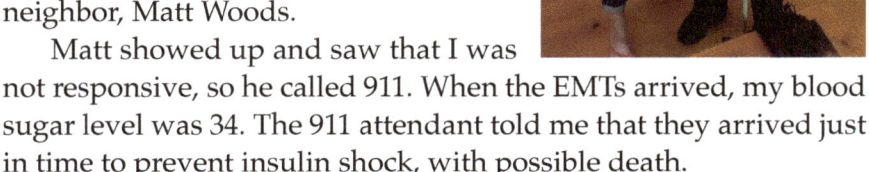

I had an appointment to call Marlene that day at 10 a.m. When she did not hear from me and I was not answering my phone, Marlene took fast action. She called my friend, Jason Housby, in Des Moines, and he got in touch with my neighbor, Matt Woods.

Matt showed up and saw that I was not responsive, so he called 911. When the EMTs arrived, my blood sugar level was 34. The 911 attendant told me that they arrived just in time to prevent insulin shock, with possible death.

Marlene stayed at my side for twelve hours. I am forever grateful and will never be able to repay Marlene, my life-saving angel.

Because of her fast action, I AM HAPPY TO BE ALIVE!

Wayne's Wisdom

Cherish every day and every friend. All friends are important. Some may even save your life.

Each morning when you open your eyes, you get two brand-new blessings: you get to open both of your eyes!

Goodbyes and Hellos

While I was finishing this book, I had to say goodbye to my dear brother B'Gene who was the last remaining member of my immediate family. B'Gene died comfortably at home in Phoenix on August 20, 2019. I was able to sit beside him and say goodbye, and a few days later I said a few words during his memorial service in Albuquerque.

On the plane ride home, as I struggled to get my luggage from an overhead storage bin, my cane hit a woman on the head. "Are you trying to get my attention?" she asked. "I am just trying out a new way to meet women," I said, with a smile.

A few weeks later, my hairdresser noticed that my eyelids were sagging into my line of vision. She suggested that I have surgery to correct that. So I had plastic surgery, and that gave me yet another way to have fun with people. The other day I walked into our post office and said to Carol Mosely, the local postmaster, "Look closely at my eyes! Now, how many ninety-nine-year-old men can you say have winked at you today?"

I have had fun with that joke many times. I have now used it on nurses, sales clerks and waitresses.

If you see someone without a smile today, give them one of yours. It may be the only sunshine they will see all day. All days are beautiful; only the weather changes.

In the time I've got left, I just want to make this world a little better. I learned that the best sermons are lived, not preached. As the saying goes, "Success is when you look back at your life and the memories make you smile."

Wayne's Wisdom

Have fun with people wherever you go. The other day a man in a store said to me, "You can't be ninety-nine years old! Let me see your driver's license!" I pulled it out and said, "Here it is, and you'll notice something else about it. It's still good for one more year, so stay out of my way!"

My Family Roots

Mayme Kilpatrick Family

*Back row: Bonnie, William Allen (Willalley), Barney, John
Middle row: Mayme, Stella, Tennessee (Tenny)
Front row: Marian (twin), Wayne's grandfather Samuel Adams,
Neva, Wayne's grandmother America Mary Lee, Mildred (twin)*

Arthur Clyde Williams Family

Left: Francis Milo and Minnie Williams. Right Top: Arthur Clyde (A.C.), Lawrence, Ralph. Right Bottom: Mildred, Eldon, Geneva (other sibling images unavailable)

Emma Jane Castledine Williams (A.C.'s mother)

Samuel Allen and America Mary Lee Kilpatrick (Mayme's parents)

A.C. and Mayme Williams

Wayne and Rosie Williams

Grandfather Francis (Milo) Williams and Wayne in 1922
Top: Signature of Milo Williams from a letter dated November 21, 1886

> *So the next generation would know,*
> *and all the generations to come—*
> *Know the truth and tell the stories*
> *so their children can trust in God,*
> *Never forget the works of God*
> *but keep his commands to the letter.*
> —*Psalm 78:6-7 (MSG)*

Getting to Know My Family

My Family

Richard's daughter Wendy, son-in-law Geoff and grandchildren Kenzie and Tate Ellis

Richard's wife Beverly with daughter Wendy and grandchildren Kenzie and Tate

Pennie's son Scott, his wife Tamara and grandchildren Bri and Emily

Pennie's son Jason

Pennie with her daughter Amber, son-in-law Johnnie and grandchildren Brenna and Bella

Pennie's daughter Amber, son-in-law Johnnie and granddaughters Brenna and Bella

Lana with her husband Steve Farmer

Bobby's daughter Amy Williams

Polly's daughter Linda, son-in-law John and grandsons Dominic, Elias and Roman

Polly's daughter Noella and grandsons Kamerynn and Khryztain with Wayne

Polly's grandsons Kamerynn and Khryztain at current age

Polly and her husband Noel

"I Choose Happy!"

For my 96th birthday, my nephew Gary wrote this poem which helps me to summarize my life philosophy and the message of this book.

> More than merely alive at age ninety-five,
> Wayne has shown that he knows how to live.
> With joy in his family, his friends and his God,
> He's been teaching us all how to give.
>
> In his eyes there's a gleam and his latest theme
> He declares is: "I'm still on a roll!"
> It's the caption he posts—a well-deserved boast.
> He has not let the years take a toll!
>
> And today to his age he adds a new page—
> He's accrued now four score and sixteen!
> Yes, Wayne's still on a roll! The number has changed,
> But his mind is still witty and keen!
>
> Wayne wrote down his mission and philosophy,
> With a focus that sets him apart.
> Why live to make money when you can instead
> Make a difference in somebody's heart?

"I want others to feel as good as I do,"
Says this active, unstoppable man.
"I'm on a mission! In what time I've left, to
Help all of the people I can."

With youth camps, churches, Know Your Bible and more
Wayne has seen what was needed, pursued,
And created until it succeeded, then
Celebrated with deep gratitude.

Friends through the years still call him often to say,
"Thank you for what you gave to my life
And the effort you made. I'm better today
Because of knowing you and your wife."

Wayne has lost parents, sister, brother, two sons,
And his wife of seventy-two years—
His beloved companion from youth. We know
He's no stranger to grief, pain or tears.

But Wayne understands, with a heart full of faith,
In the end what seemed loss will be gain.
That there's more to his story, and joy ahead.
He will see those he loves once again.

"When I woke up this morning, I had a choice:
I could be either happy or sad.
I chose happy!" Wayne says, and there in his voice
You hear all that you need to feel glad.

"I have moments when I am grouchy," he adds,
"But this isn't one … And it's true
You can't make me mad, because I've decided
That I am kinda fond of you."

"We're not getting younger. Let's get together!"
Says this man who loves to connect.
"This is one of my feisty days!" he responds
When you ask. What else would you expect?

He meets life with a grin and glows from within,
And if you want to see him turn loose
Just ask him to talk about something he loves—
For example, his mangosteen juice!

As this world goes insane, one thing is quite plain:
There are many who don't know the way.
Everyone would be better if they just knew Wayne
And lived like he lives every day.

Sayings I Like

- Deep within each person is an intense desire to feel strong, effective, powerful and in control of his or her life. You automatically trigger that feeling of self-confidence and self-esteem when you start to work on the task that is most important to you at the moment.

  —Shobha Lyer

- When we depart this world all that matters is not how much money we have made or the possessions we have. What matters are the lives we have touched, the love we have shown, and the memories we have made.

  —Author Unknown

- So many people come into our lives and then leave the way they came, but there are these precious few who touch our heart so deeply we will never be the same.

  —Flavia Wooden

- You may not think the world needs you but it does. For you are unique, like no one that has ever been before you or will come after. No one can speak with your voice, say your piece, smile your smile or shine your light. No one can take your place for it is yours alone to fill. If you are not there to shine your light, who knows how many travelers will lose their way as they try to pass by your empty place in the darkness.

  —Lawrence and Hazel Mahar

- No amount of darkness can smother out the light of a single candle.

  —*St. Francis of Assisi*

- Everything you need is already inside of you. Do not wait for others to light your fire. You already have your own matches.

  —*Darren Hardy*

- Be kind and merciful. Let no one ever come to you without coming away better and happier.

  —*Mother Teresa*

A Few Plaques from Wayne's Walls

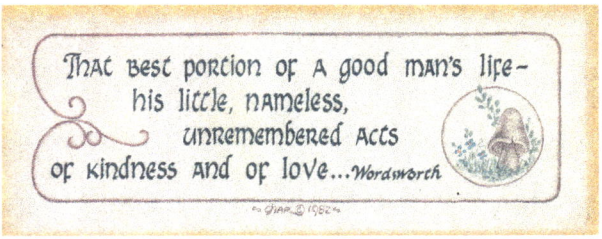

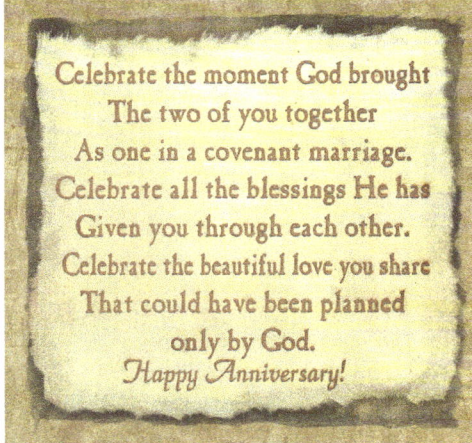

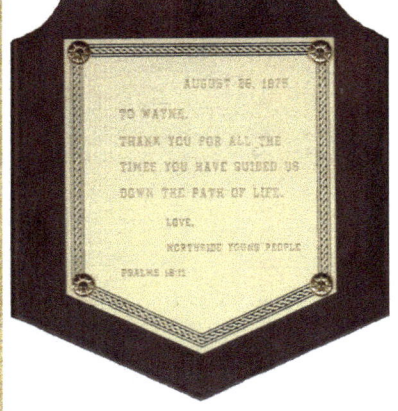

Thank You!

Thank you for reading this and for letting me share my story with you.

Many people worked together to help me create this book. It is the result of marvelous teamwork and several people deserve special mention.

I want to thank Marlene Brice for her wonderful friendship. She gave me a powerful little book, *The Simple Truths of Appreciation* by Barbara Glanz, and that started the thinking process that led to me writing this book. It also led to my friendship with Barbara Glanz whose generous kindness, encouragement and suggestions have improved this book.

Geoff and Wendy Ellis assumed key responsibilities which were vital to help me complete this book and get it into your hands. Bonnie's daughters, Lorraine Brock and Vicki Livingston, provided crucial support that made this book possible. Wendy, Lorraine and Vicki also made many valuable suggestions which improved what I wrote. With Vicki's daughter, AnnaLee, they gathered and added many photos which enriched the book and helped me to show off several generations. I am incredibly grateful for each of them. Richard's wife, Beverly Williams; Bobby's wife, Diane Williams, and their daughter, Amy Williams; and my children, Pennie, Lana and Polly, also corrected errors and provided valuable details. All of them have helped me through the years in many other invaluable ways.

Marlys McFerren, my friend for many years, gave me wonderful proofreading and suggestions. From the beginning, Jason

Housby has helped me with invaluable planning, technical support and in editing and preparing photos. This book would have been impossible for me to complete without Jason and my nephew, Gary Williams, who served as my editor.

Lisa Livingston McSpadden, Vicki's daughter, donated her skills as a professional photographer and took my photo for the front cover of this book, as well as one on the back cover. Learn about her at: www.lisamacphotography.com.

The cap that I am wearing proudly in the cover photo was a gift from my niece, Kathy Thomas, and her husband, Randy, for my ninety-ninth birthday. The back of the cap reads, "Hi, I'm Uncle Wayne," which is how I often introduce myself.

My life has been deeply enriched by all of my brothers and sisters in Christ Jesus in each of the church families where I have been blessed to be a member. Besides my earthly family, I have found and adopted into my life other families—my church families, business families and friendship families—and they have adopted me into theirs! I love them all!

Finally, my thanks also to the nice people at Telemachus Press —especially Steve Himes and MaryAnn Nocco— for their expertise and professionalism.

Wayne's Wisdom

Creating this book has been a wonderful experience for me. Now that you have read it, I challenge you to do what I have done. You too have a story to tell. Please share it with the world. Doing that will bless you and all the people you love.

Wayne's Mission Statement And Philosophy For His Life On This Earth
Written February 22, 2018

I will each and every day constantly make an effort to keep my life attuned to God's will for my life and will put Him first in everything I do.

I will use the talents that have been given to me (from a higher source) to share with others to see the wonderful blessings of a strong Christian life.

I have been given the ability to make a difference for the better in the lives of those I come in contact with each and every day.

This is my time in life to share with others the outstanding opportunity they have to experience better health and improved finances.

I am so blessed to be surrounded by very important close friends such as Marlene Brice and others who are of the same mind. My bro Bill, Marlene and Ron started me on this journey back in 2006, twelve years ago. I have experienced such good health since.

I choose to be gentle, compassionate, considerate, patient and generous. I choose to speak well of other people crossing my path.

I am learning as I speak and am growing in wisdom. I am in control of my destiny. Outside forces do not have a hold on me.

I do not choose to be a common man. I seek opportunity, not security.

I want to take the calculated risk, to dream, and build, to fall, make mistakes and rebound with success.

I prefer the challenges of life to a guaranteed existence. I look forward to the thrill of fulfillment and success over all odds.

The amount I earn is irrelevant. The outcomes of my life are determined by my actions.

I am choosing what I can achieve through reading and self affirmation.

I am making decisions, cutting off other possibilities and I am doing so in writing to stay the course and to avoid being double minded.

I desire to be focused, dependable and trustworthy.

It is my heritage to stand erect, proud and unafraid, to think for myself, and to enjoy the benefits of my creation.

I am always willing to go the extra mile—and when it comes time for me to depart this world, I want to announce proudly,

This I have done...

"The Optimist"

"Why live to one hundred?" asked my friend.
"Isn't ninety enough to make a good end?"
"I think of the things I would miss," I replied,
"If, at ninety, I stopped and simply died."

Thousands of mornings to see the sun rise
In a glorious blaze in the eastern skies.
Moons to wax and wane anew,
Trillions of stars in the midnight blue.

Ten springs to see the lilacs bloom
As their fragrance drifts across my room.
To see new leaves on the maple tree
As the birds return and sing to me.

Ten summers to feel the ocean breeze
As whales cavort in blue-green seas,
To watch the hawks on the thermals rise
Into the blue of summer skies.

Ten more harvests to celebrate
Of apple and peach and pear and date.
To anticipate the vintner's wines
From fresh new grapes on ancient vines.

I Choose Happy

Ten more autumns in which to see
The change of color on every tree,
Russets and golds and reds ablaze
To brighten the ever-shortening days.

Ten winters of freshly fallen snow
On mountains above and valleys below.
Of cherry-cheeked children on skis and sleds,
Of blazing hearths and soft warm beds.

Ten Christmas seasons of church bells rung,
Of mince pies eaten and carols sung.
Of families gathered to celebrate
The wonder of that age-old date.

Ten more New Years to welcome in,
To wonder what the year will bring.
Will there be a new baby for me to see?
A great-grandchild on my family tree?

I strive for another decade of living,
Of hoping and praying and loving and giving.
And, if I reach one hundred, what then?
Why, I'd plan to live to one hundred and ten!

Poem by Beryl MacDonald in Keizer, Oregon, age 91
From a Dear Annie column posted October 10, 2019.
Thanks to Barbara Glanz, who shared it with me and said, "Wayne, this is YOU!"

Lord, You take over. I'm about to die, my life an offering on God's altar. This is the only race worth running. I've run hard right to the finish, believed all the way. All that's left now is the shouting—God's applause! Depend on it, he's an honest judge. He'll do right not only by me, but by everyone eager for his coming.

—2 Timothy 4:6 (MSG)

Postscript

Errol Wayne Williams died peacefully in his sleep in a care facility in Wichita, Kansas, on March 29, 2020. He was ninety-nine years old.